I0493008

Vegan Hearts

Coloring Book

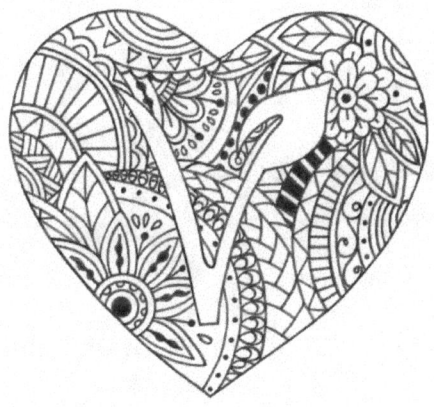

Over 25 hand-drawn unique, stress relieving hearts with doodles to color, relax, and enjoy!

Maritza Oliver

COLOR ME FREE BOOKS
British Columbia, Canada

Vegan Logo Credited:

Retrieved from www.vegansociety.com

Copyright © 2016 Maritza Oliver

All rights reserved.

International Standard Book Number

ISBN 13: 978-1535113168

Formatting & Cover Design by Maritza Oliver

Printed in the United States, Charleston SC

Hello, welcome to my book!

I created this special edition of *Vegan Hearts Coloring Book* as one of the perks I offered in addition to pre-ordering my new children's book *A Pig IS a Dog IS a Kid*. Unlike most coloring books, which are computer generated and mass produced, I decided to make my own version especially for you for being so awesome and kind to animals: over 25 hand-drawn illustrations of vegan hearts. Accompanying each drawing is an inspiring animal rights quote.

I have not printed the drawings on both sides of the pages in case you want to cut the artwork out and use the coloured hearts as greeting cards, postcards, frame them to admire, keep or give away. The possibilities are endless!

Coloring is not just an activity for keeping kids occupied. Coloring can be therapeutic, and creating beautiful art is a soothing and stress-relieving activity. So just relax, be calm, and color your vegan heart!

I hope you enjoy coloring this book as much as I enjoyed making it.

Thank you for your support!

Maritza Oliver

Tester Page

Try your materials first. Try out your coloring techniques here!

"The greatness of a nation and its moral progress can be judged by the way its animals are treated."

-Gandhi-

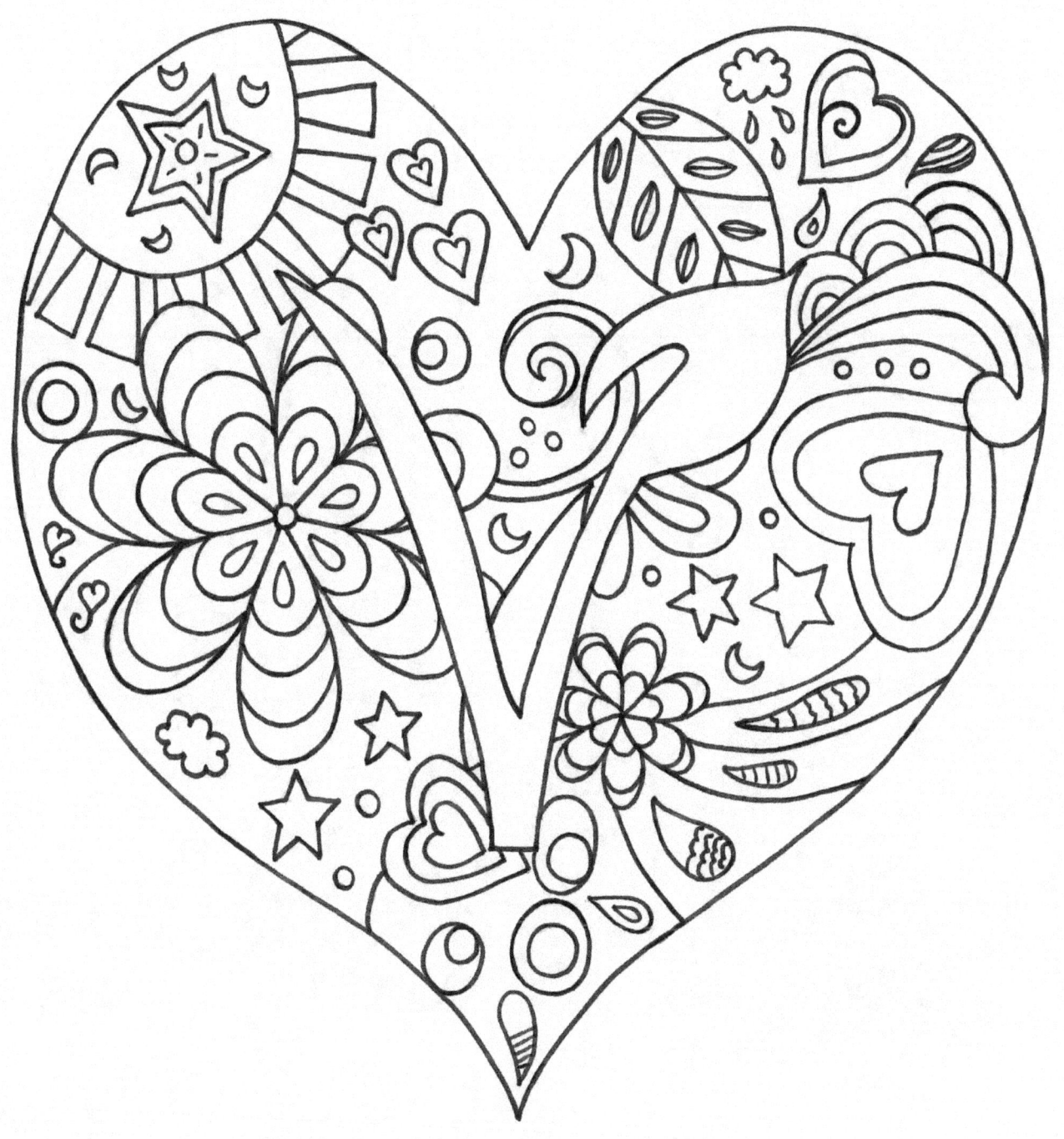

"Never doubt that a small group of thoughtful, committed people can change the world. Indeed, it is the only thing that ever has." -Margaret Mead

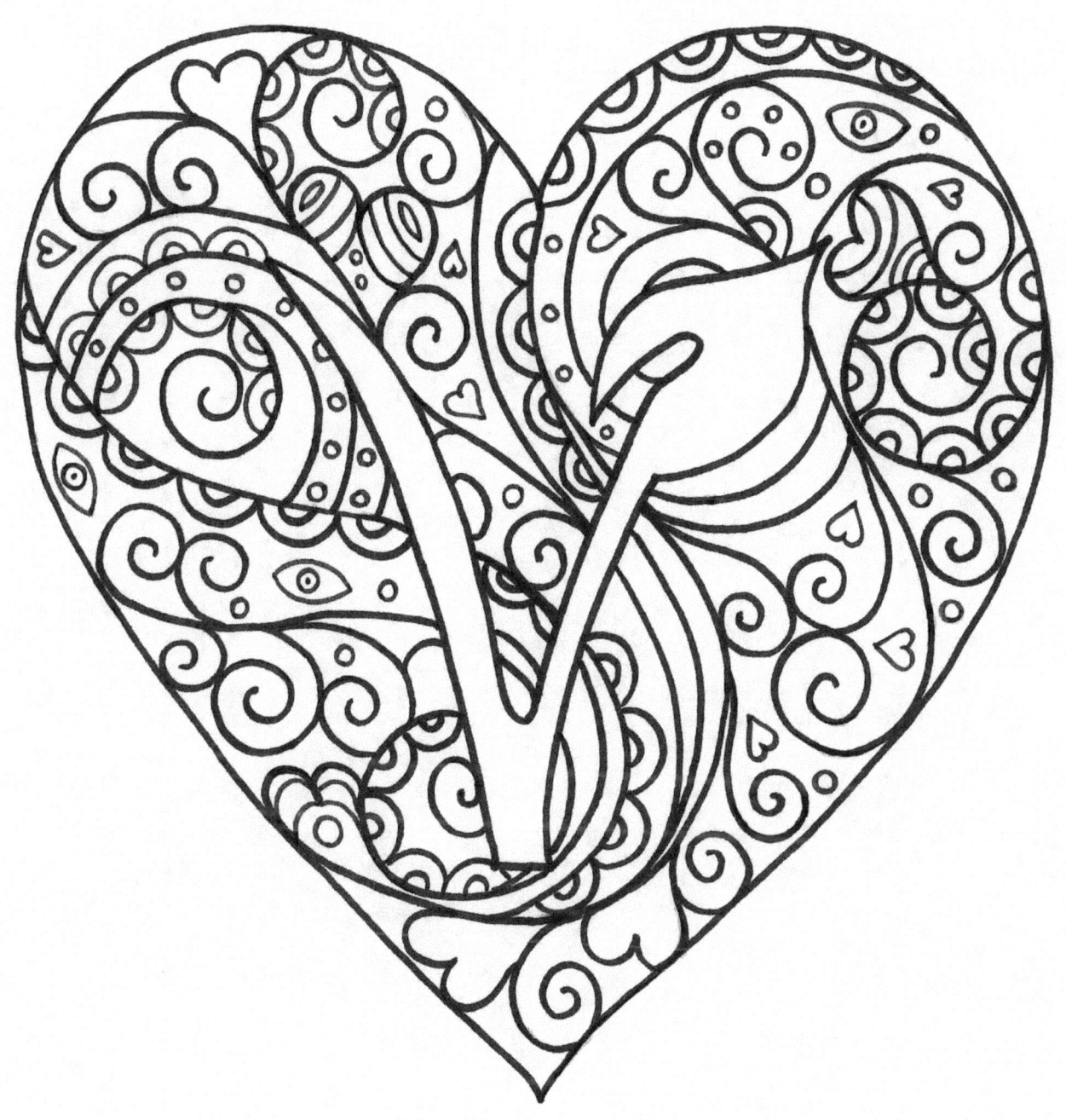

"Unless someone like you cares a whole awful lot nothing is going to get better."

-Dr. Seuss-

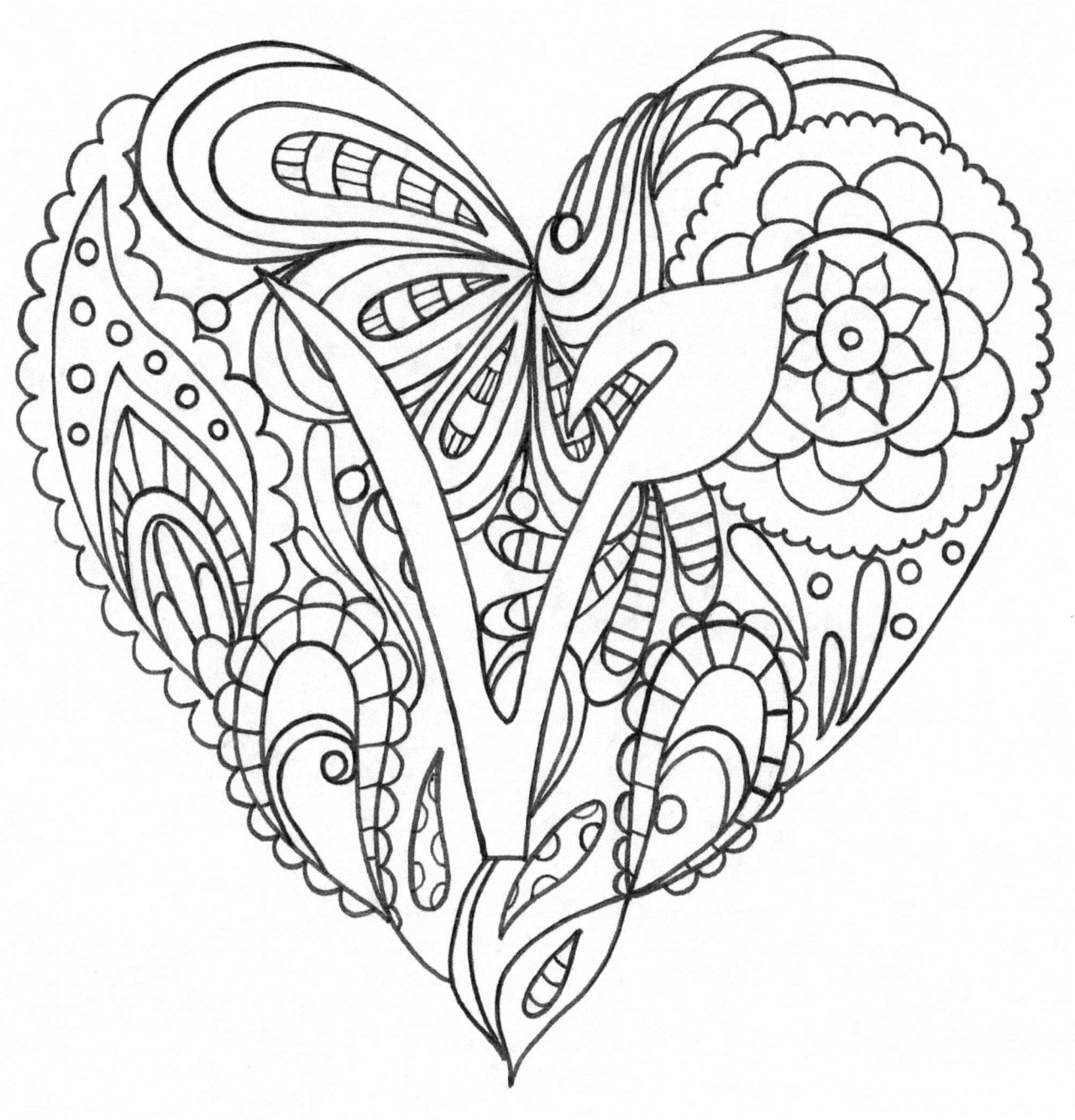

"We must always take sides. Neutrality helps the oppressor, never the victim."

-Ellie Wiesel

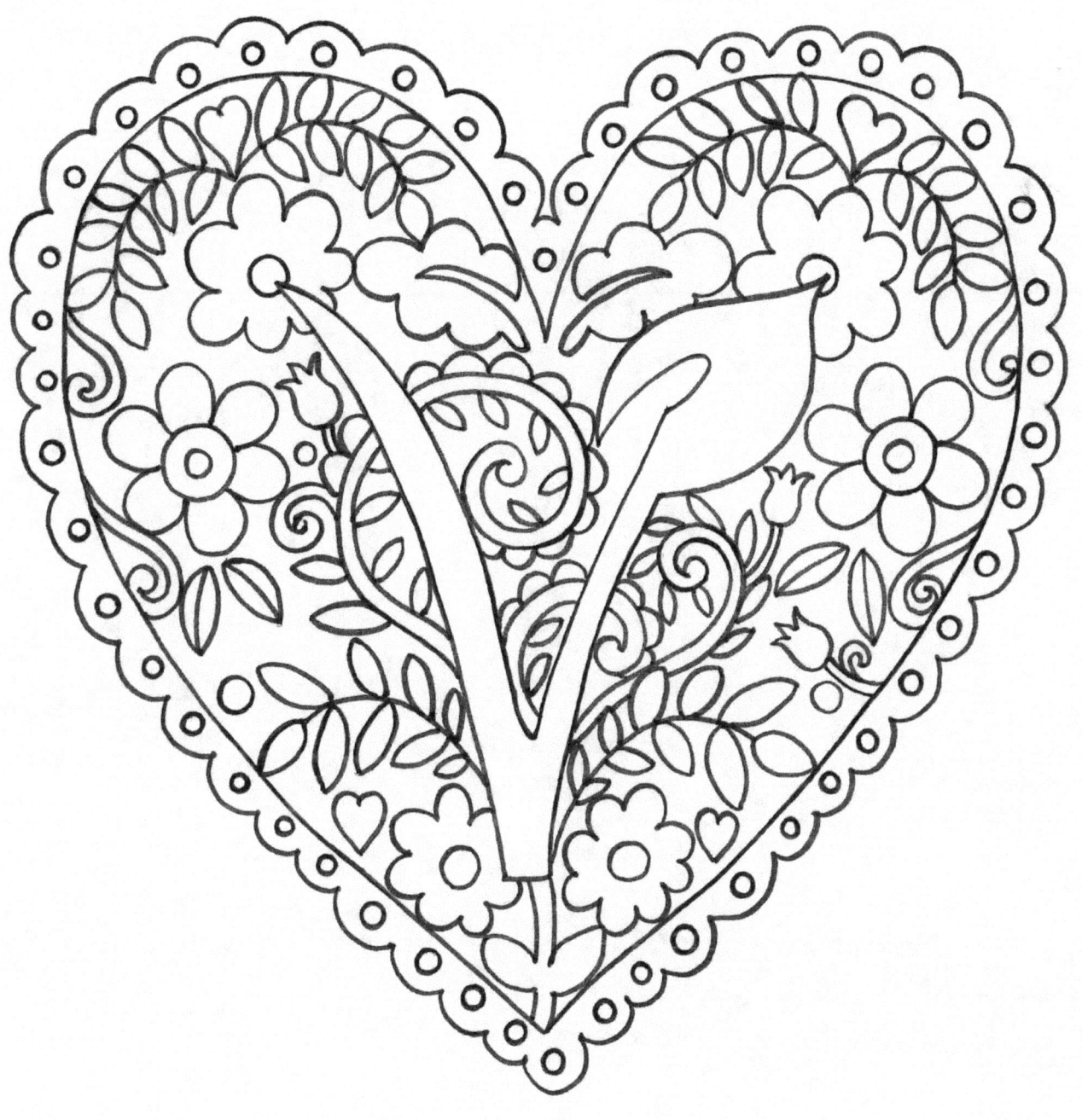

"He who is cruel to animals becomes hard also in his dealings with men. We can judge the heart of a man by his treatment of animals." -Immanuel Kant

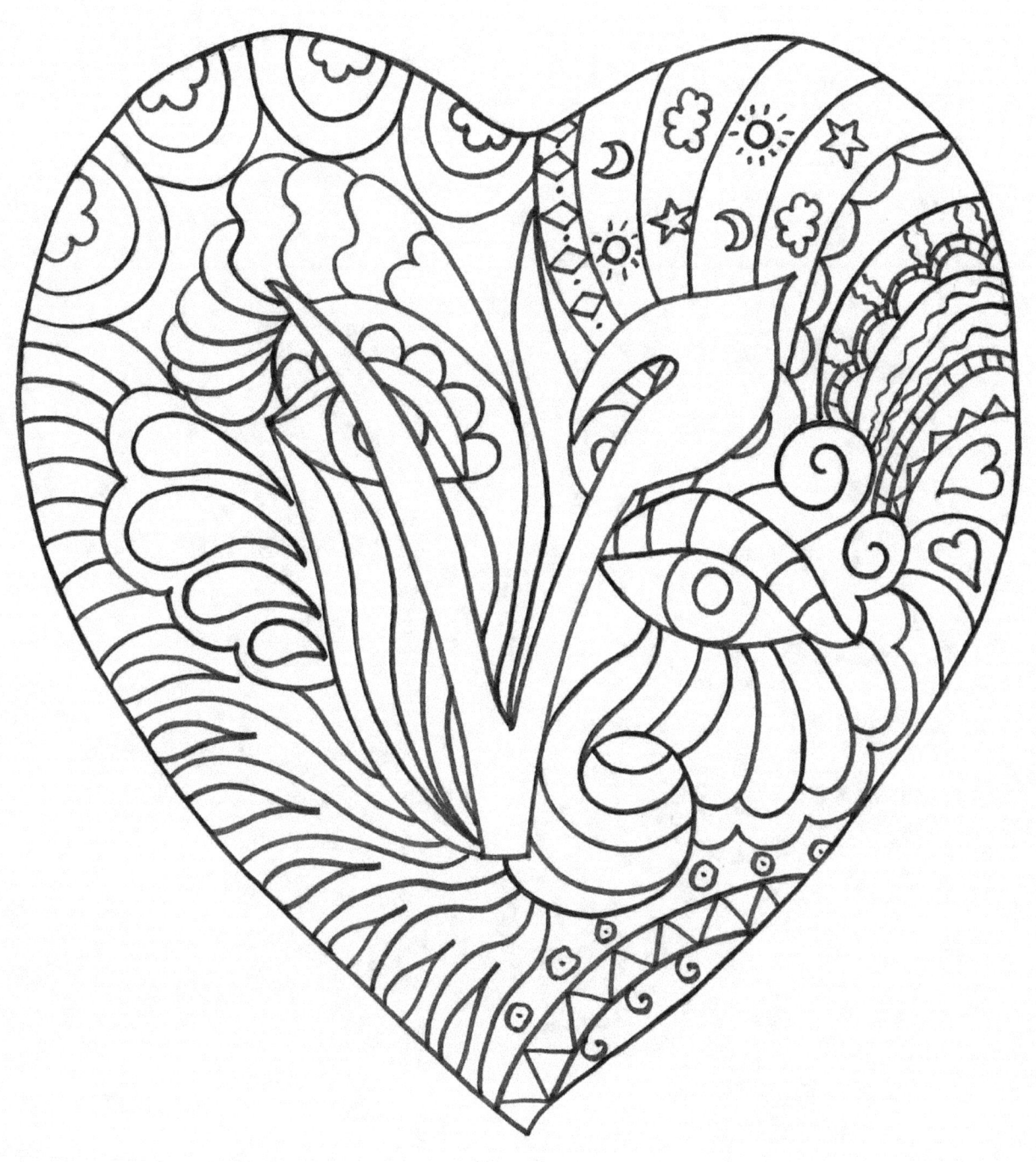

"The question is not, "Can they reason?" nor, "Can they talk?" but "Can they suffer?"

-Jeremy Bentham-

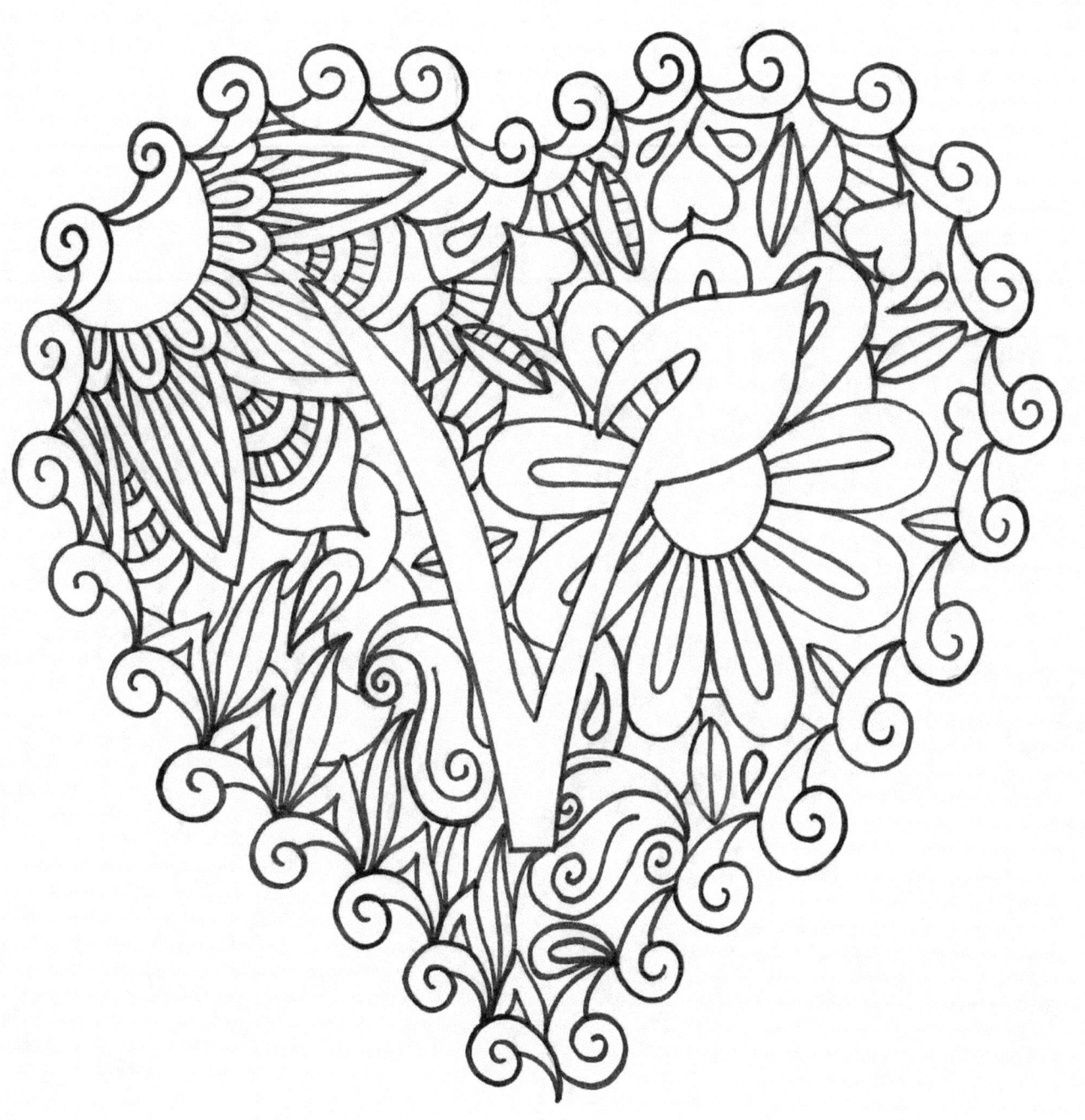

"The time will come when men such as I will look upon the murder of animals as they now look on the murder of men."
-Leonardo da Vinci"

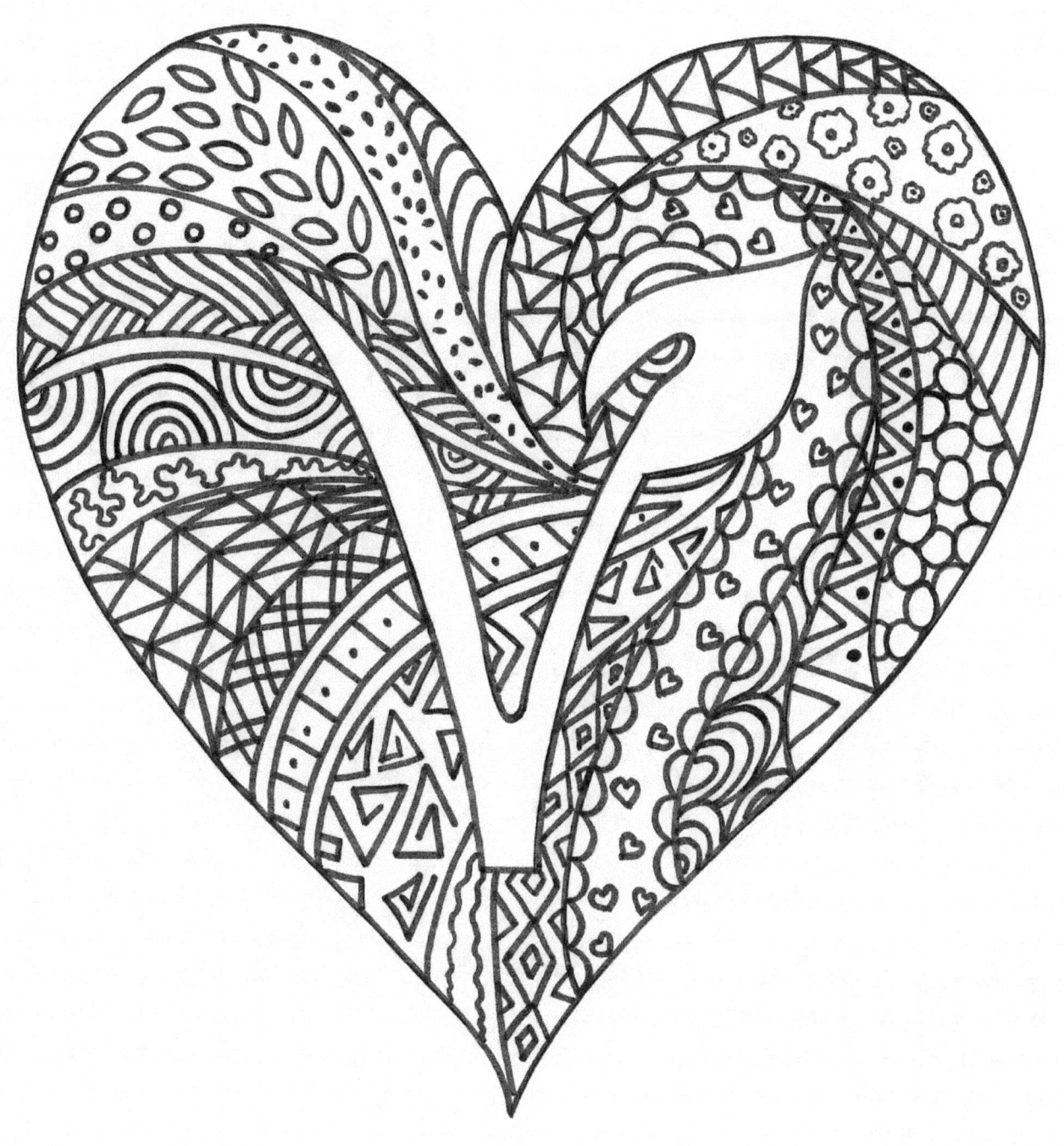

"We know we cannot be kind to animals until we stop exploiting them in the name of science, sport, fashion, and yes, in the name of food." -Cesar Chavez

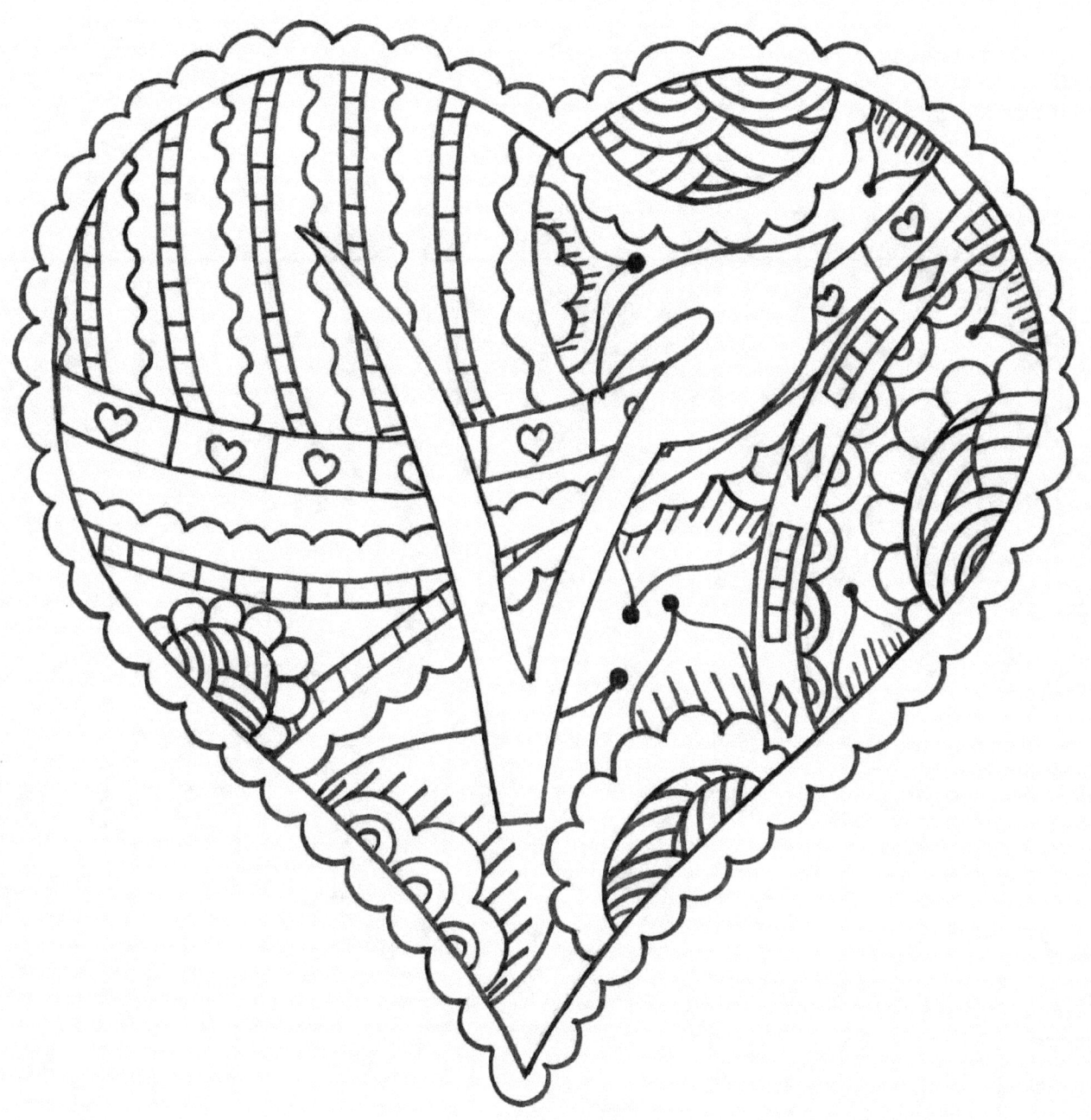

"If possessing a higher degree of intelligence does not
entitle one human to use another for his or her own ends,
how can it entitle humans to exploit non-humans?"
– Peter Singer-

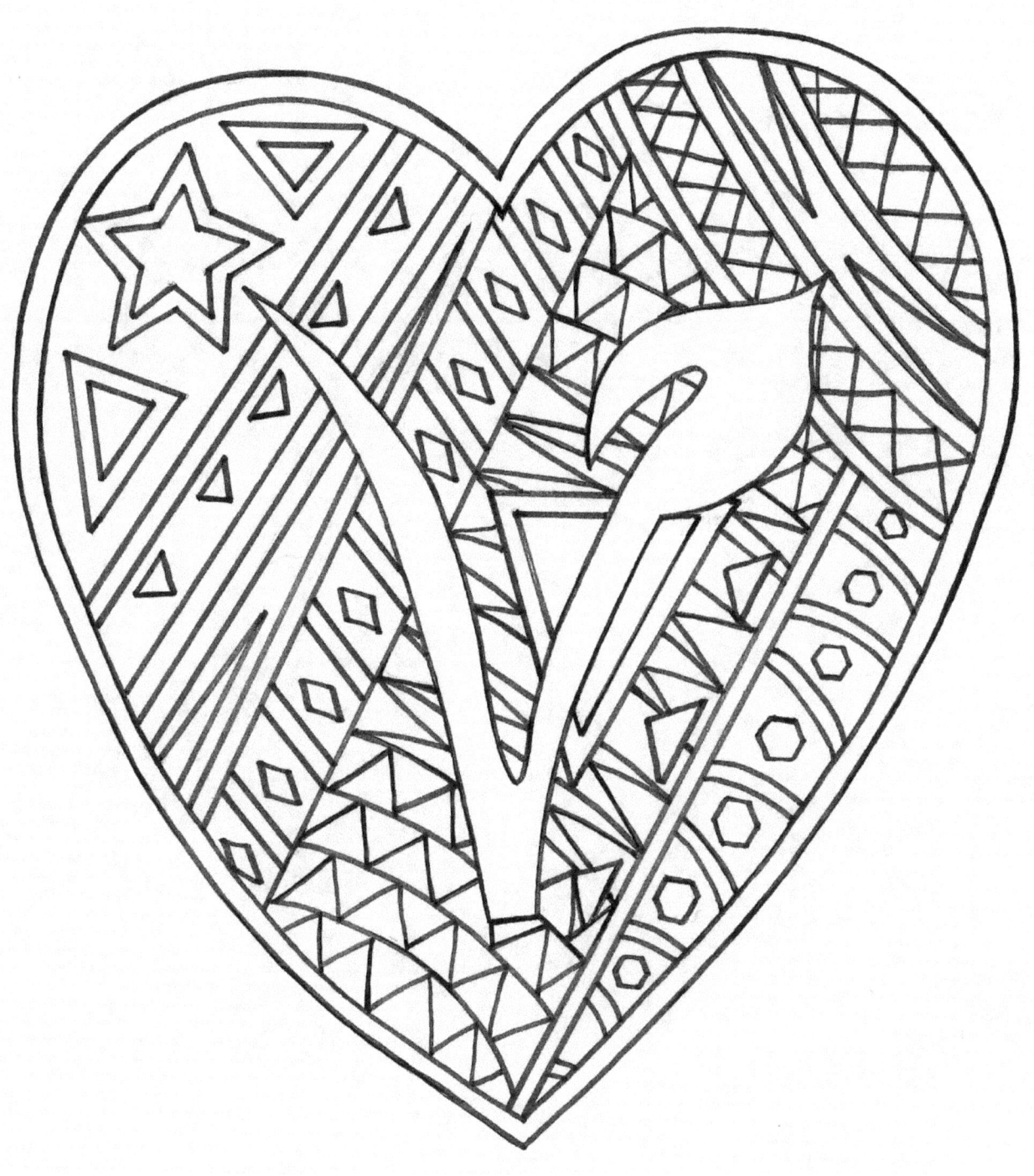

"Know that the same spark of life that is within you, is within all of our animal friends, the desire to live is the same within all of us." -Rai Aren

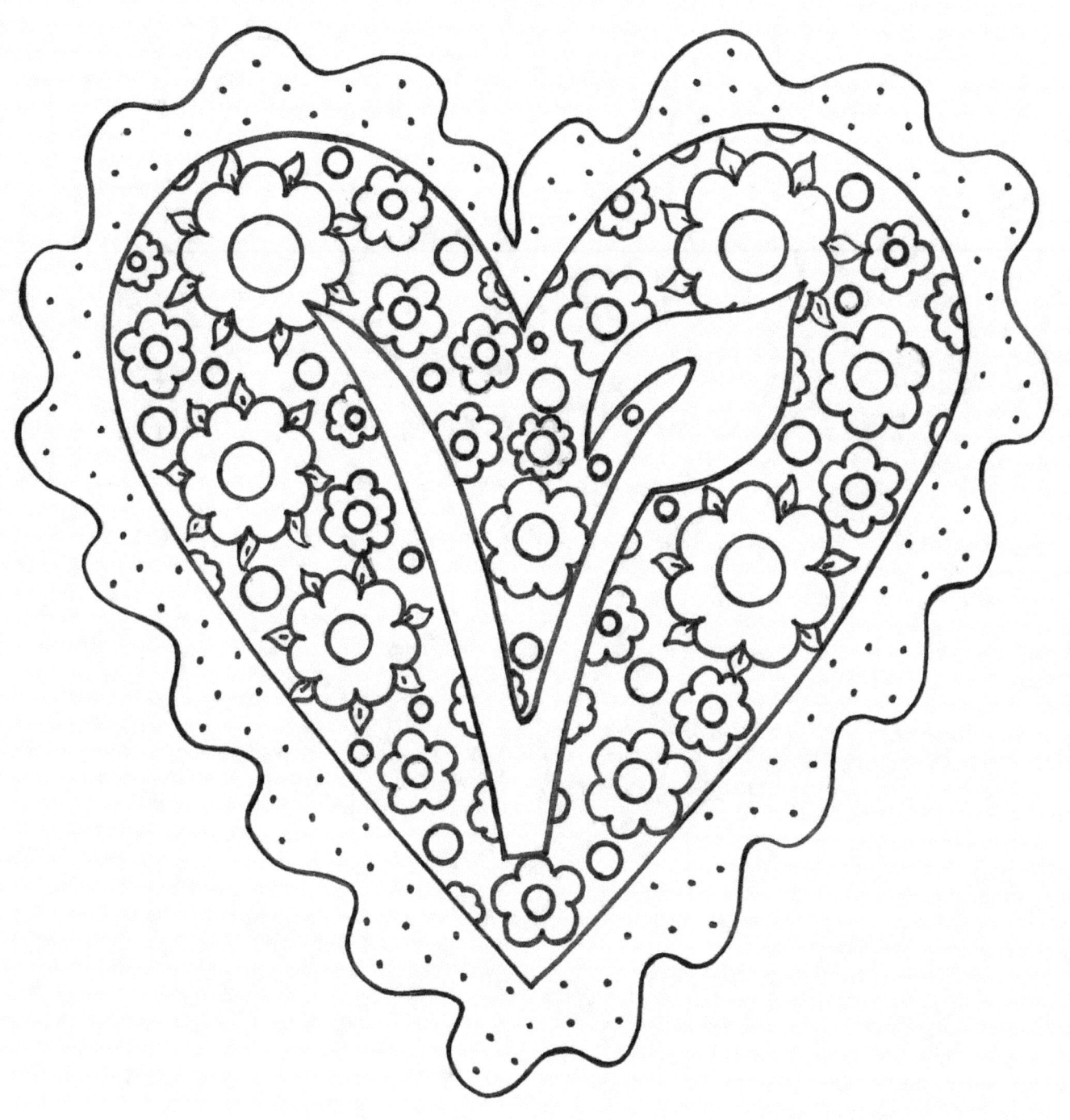

"Humanity's true moral test, its fundamental test... consists
of its attitude towards those who are at its mercy:
animals." -Milan Kundera

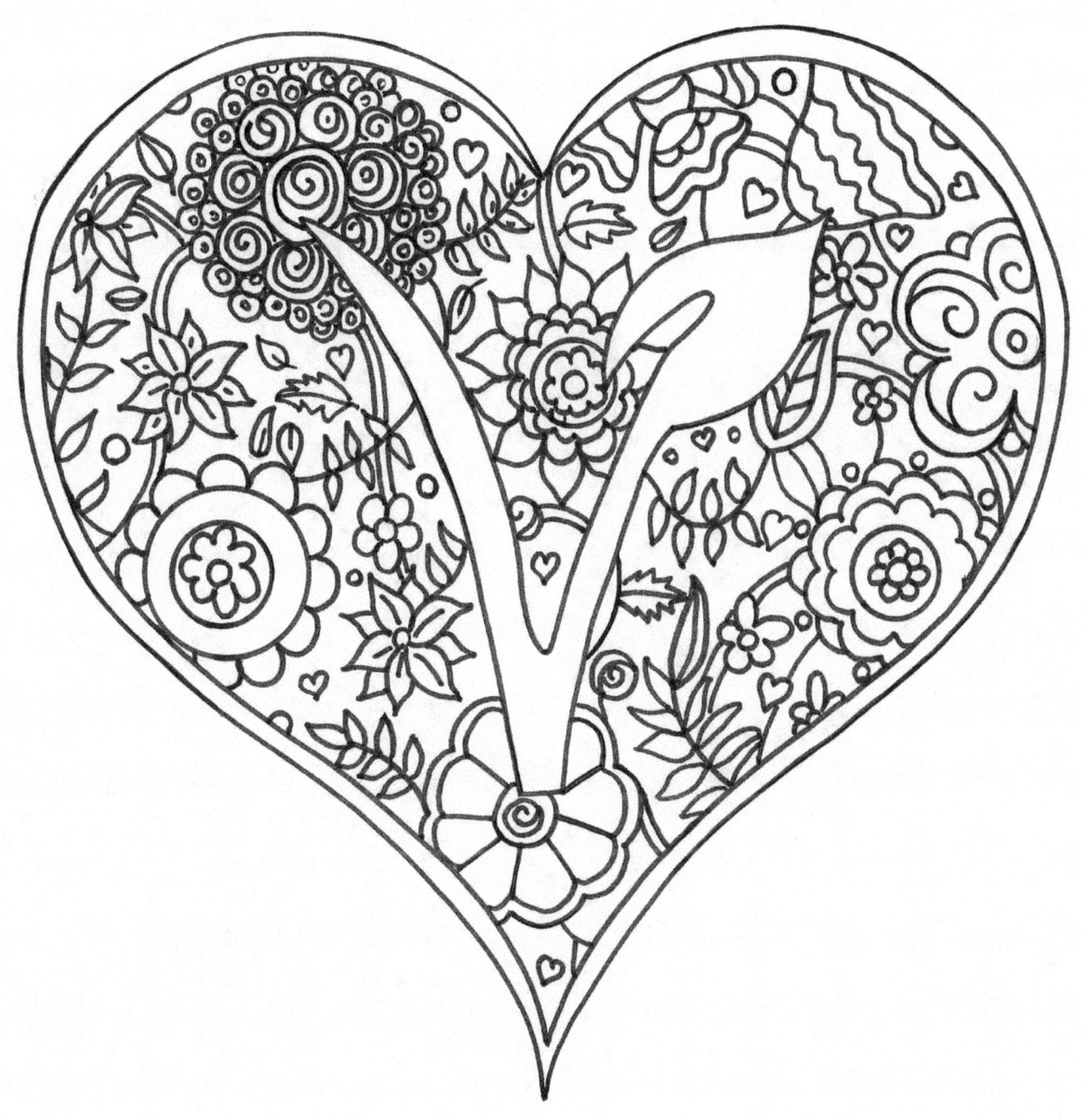

"Only when we have become nonviolent towards all life will

we have learned to live well with others."

-Cesar Chavez-

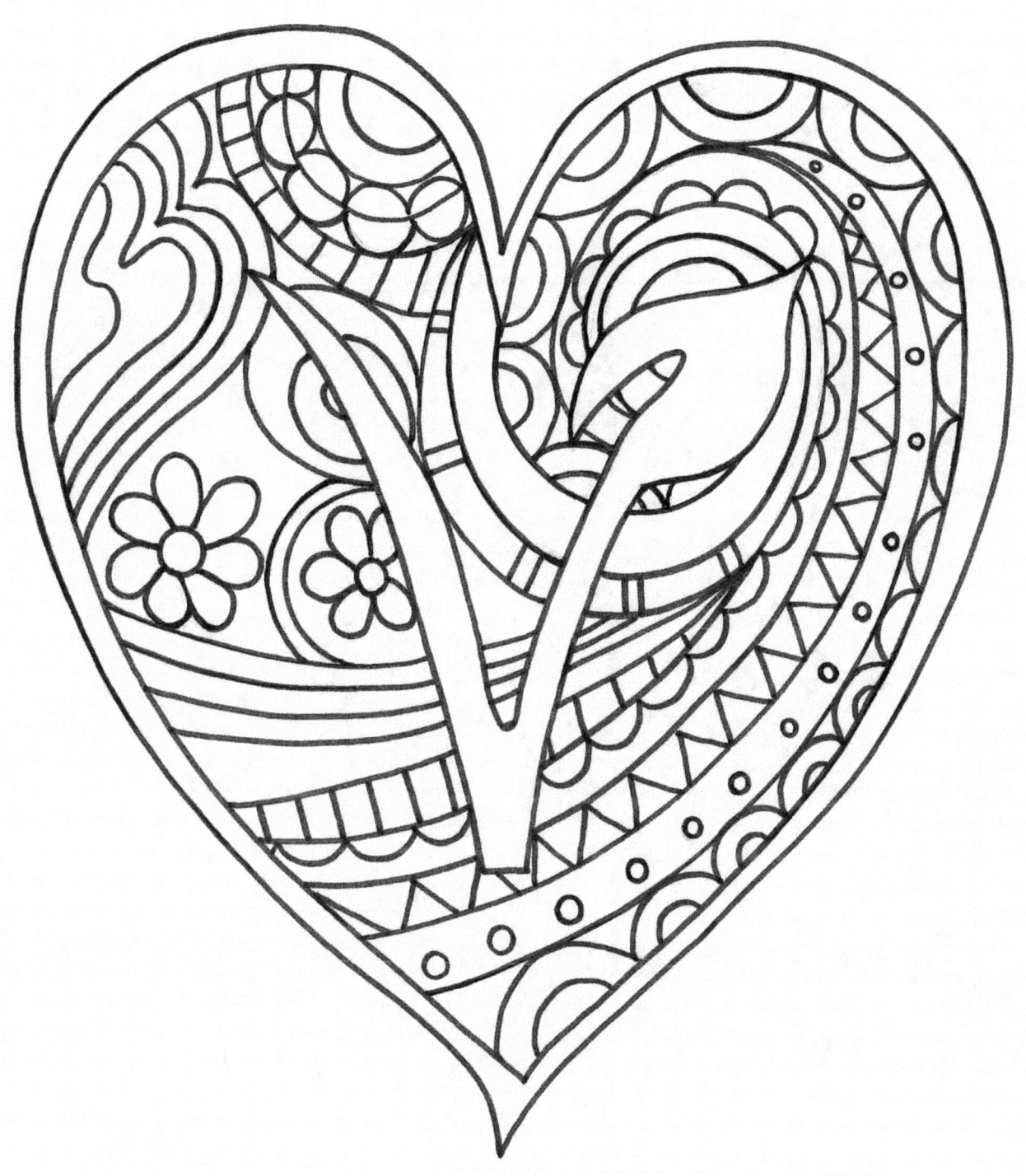

"Not responding is a response –we are equally responsible for what we don't do."

-Jonathan Safran Foer-

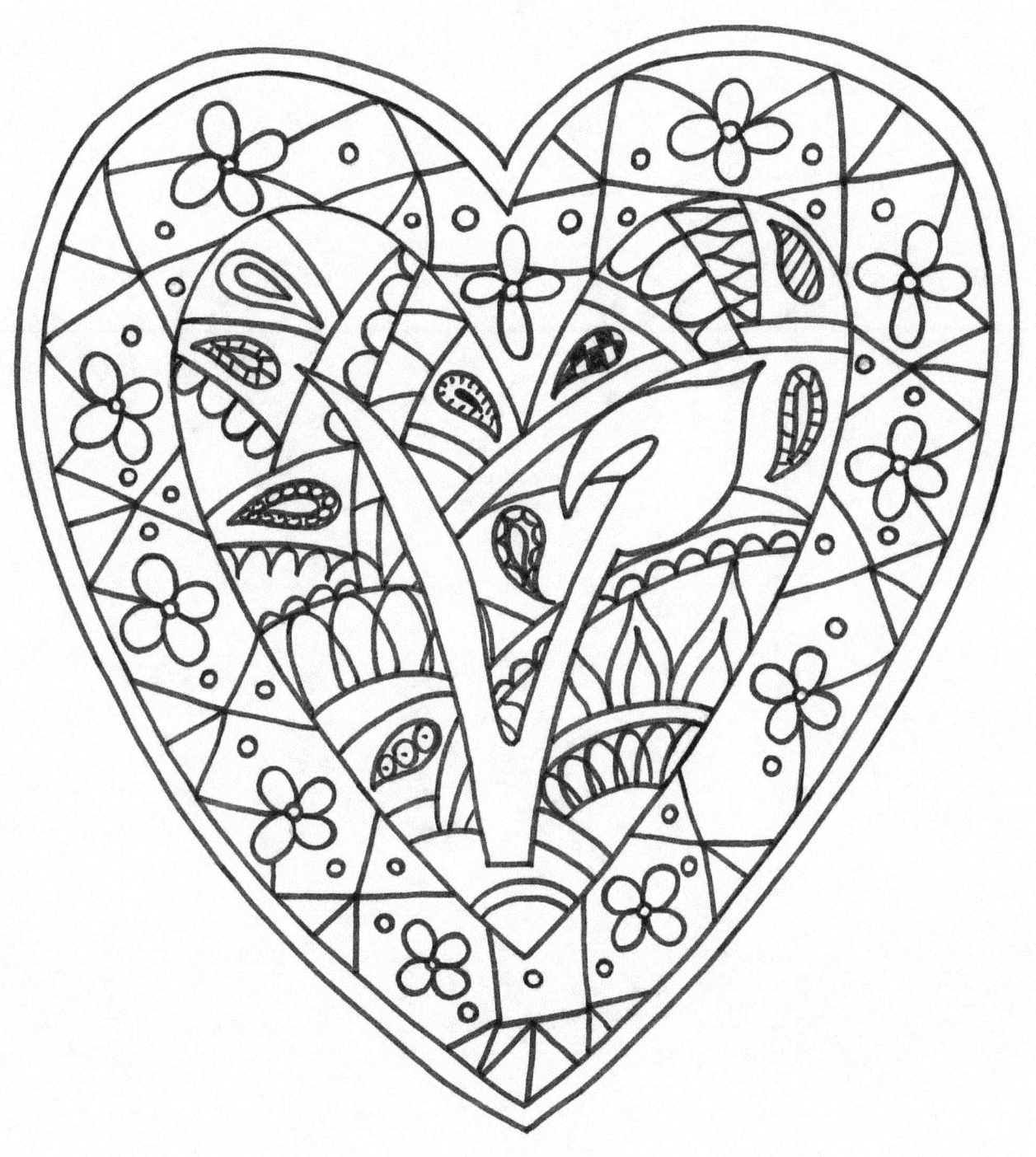

"Often, the greater our ignorance about something", the greater our resistance to change."

-Mark Beoff-

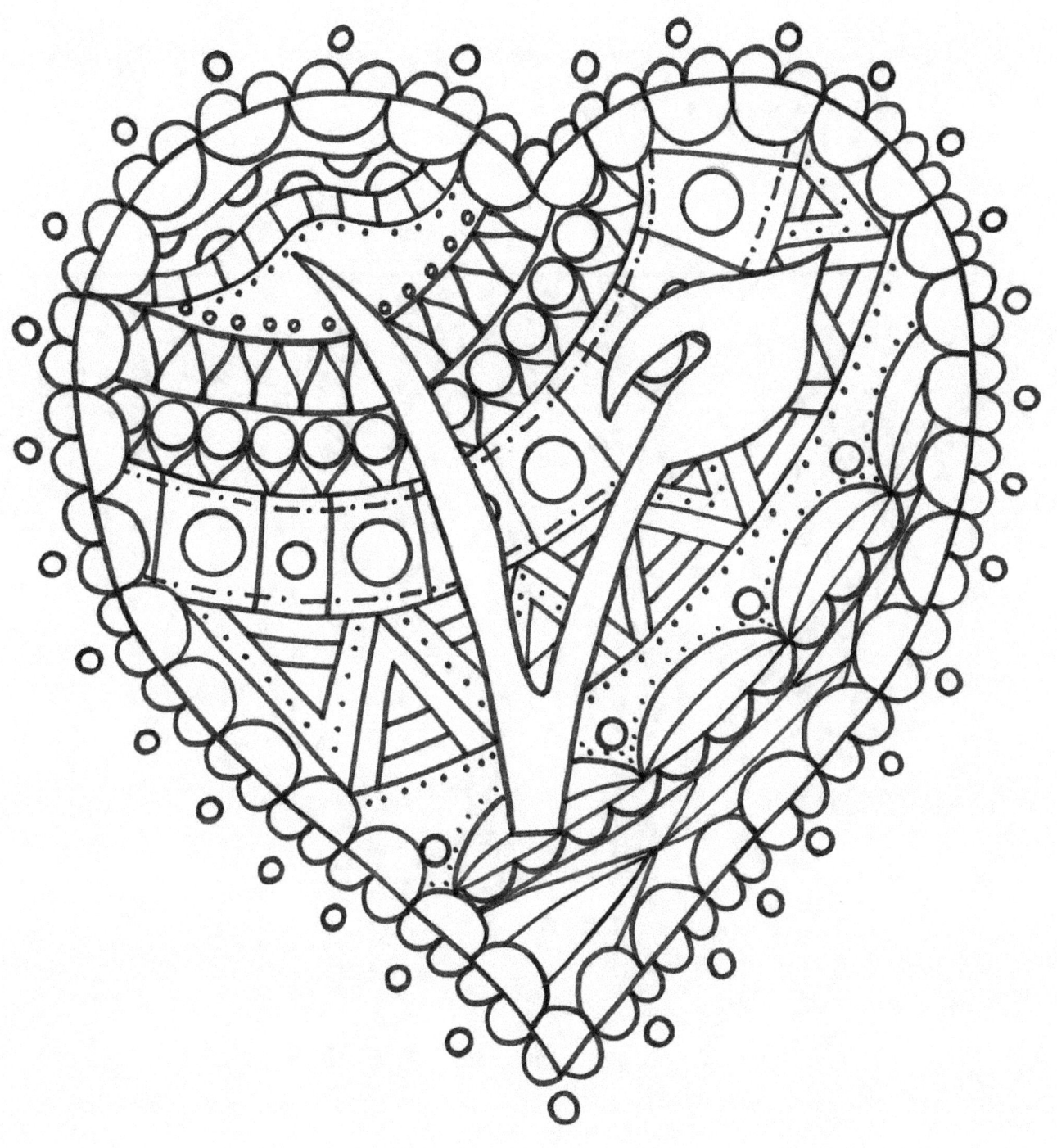

"Animals can communicate quite well. And they do. And generally speaking, they are ignored."

-Alice Walker"

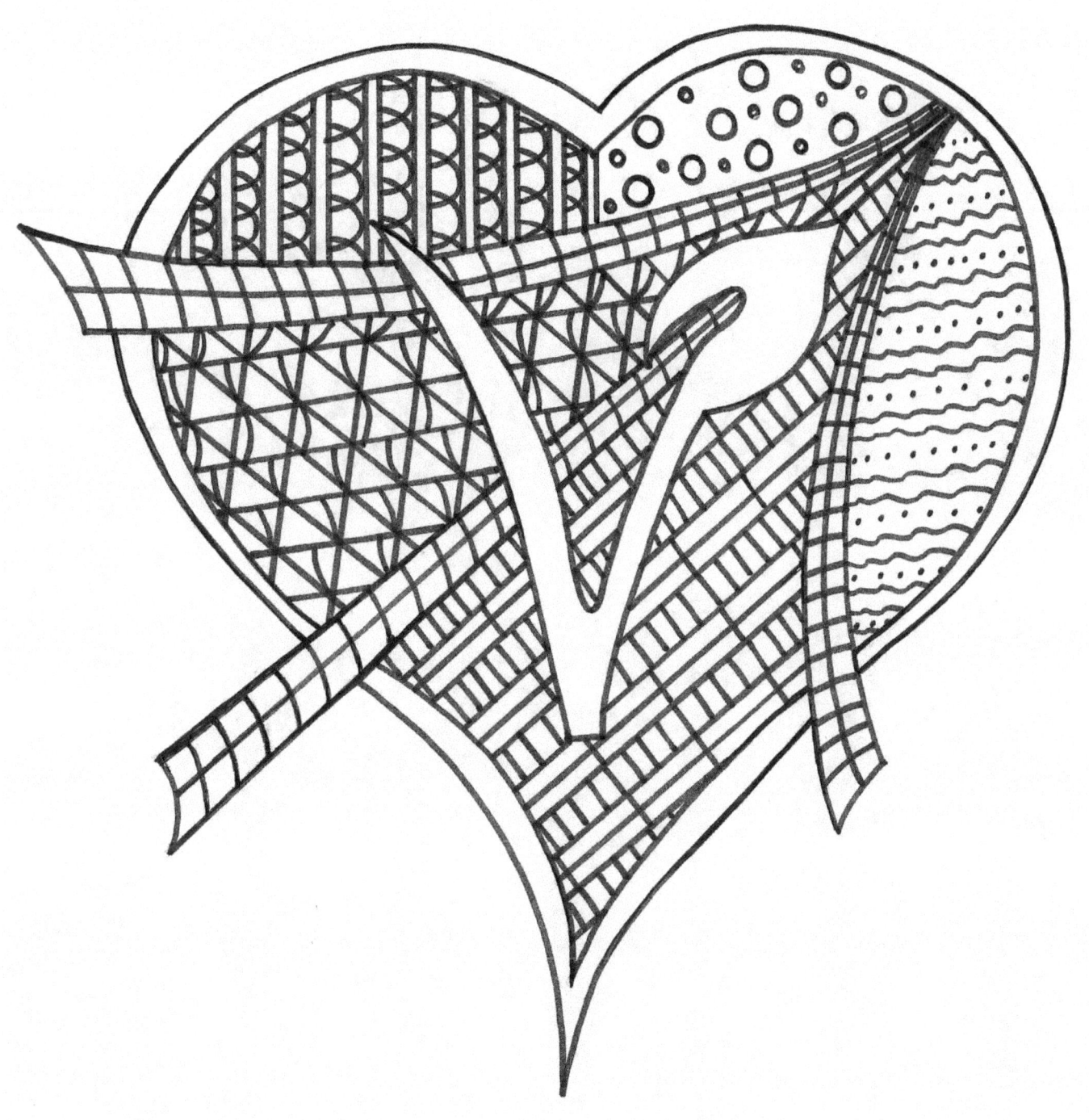

"Becoming vegan is the most important and direct change we can immediately make to save the planet and its species." -Chris Hedges

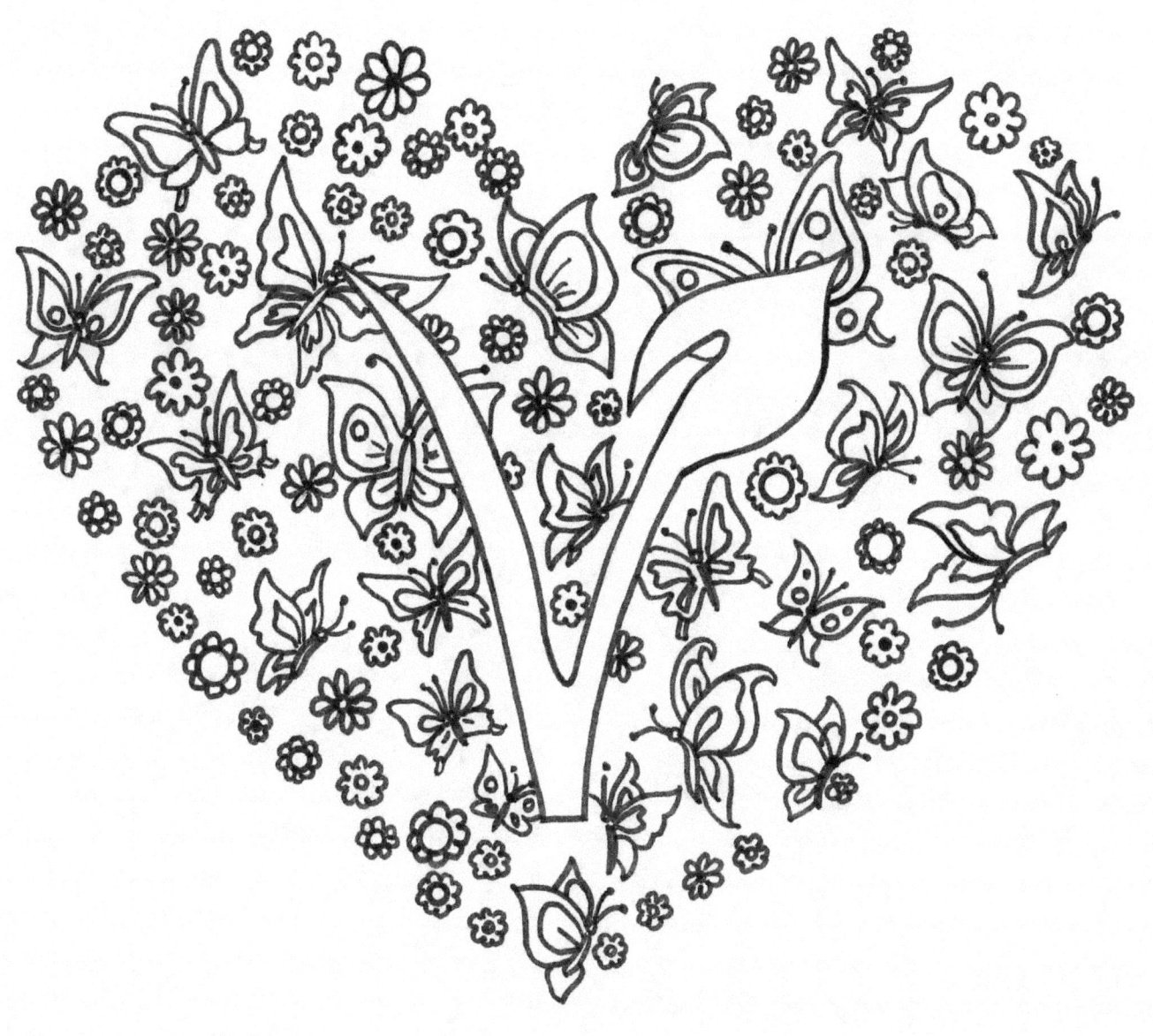

"We need another and wiser and perhaps a more mystical concept of animals... They are not our brethren; they are not underlings; they are other nations, caught with ourselves in the net of life." -Henry Beston

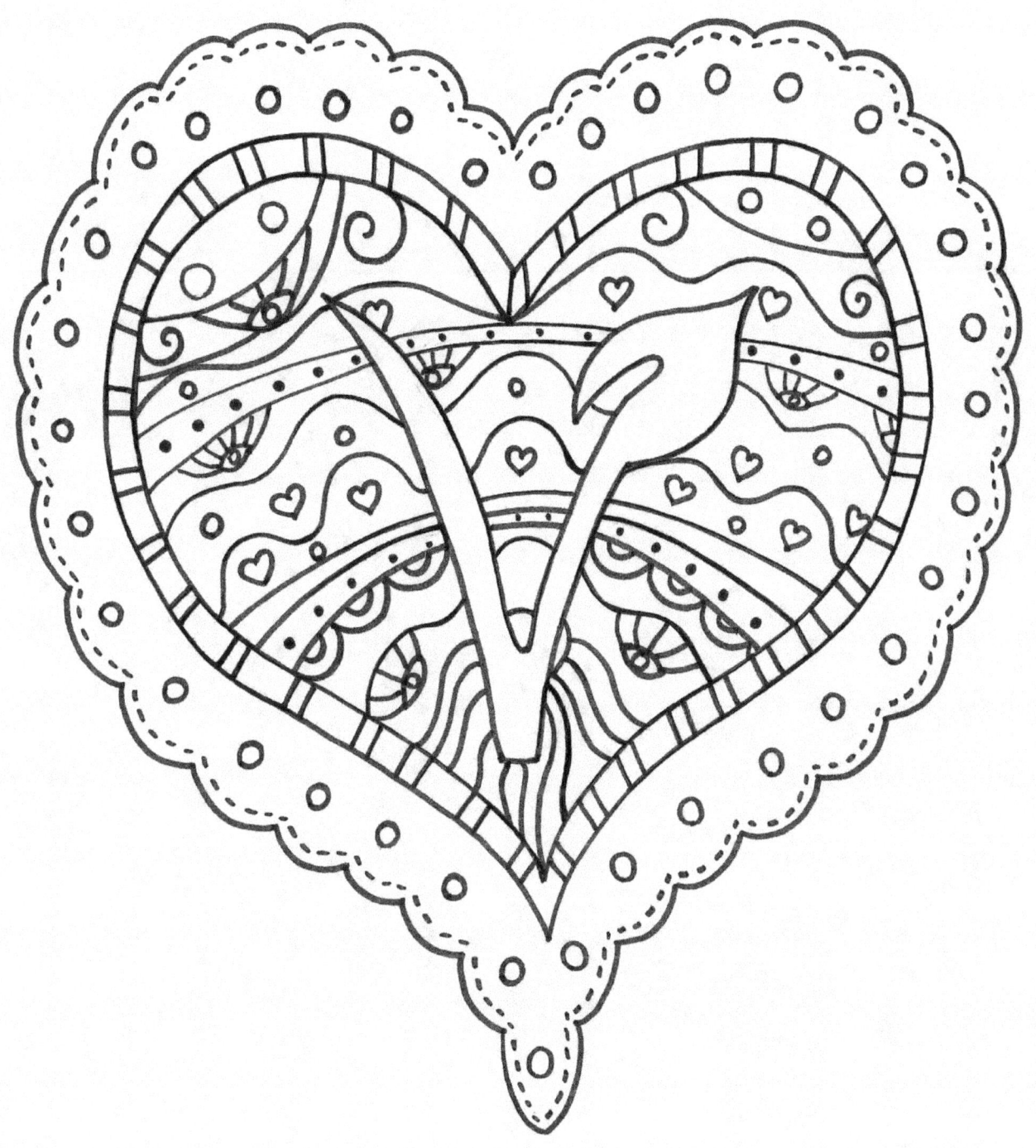

"Teaching a child not to step on a caterpillar is as valuable
to the child as it is to the caterpillar."

-Bradley Miller"

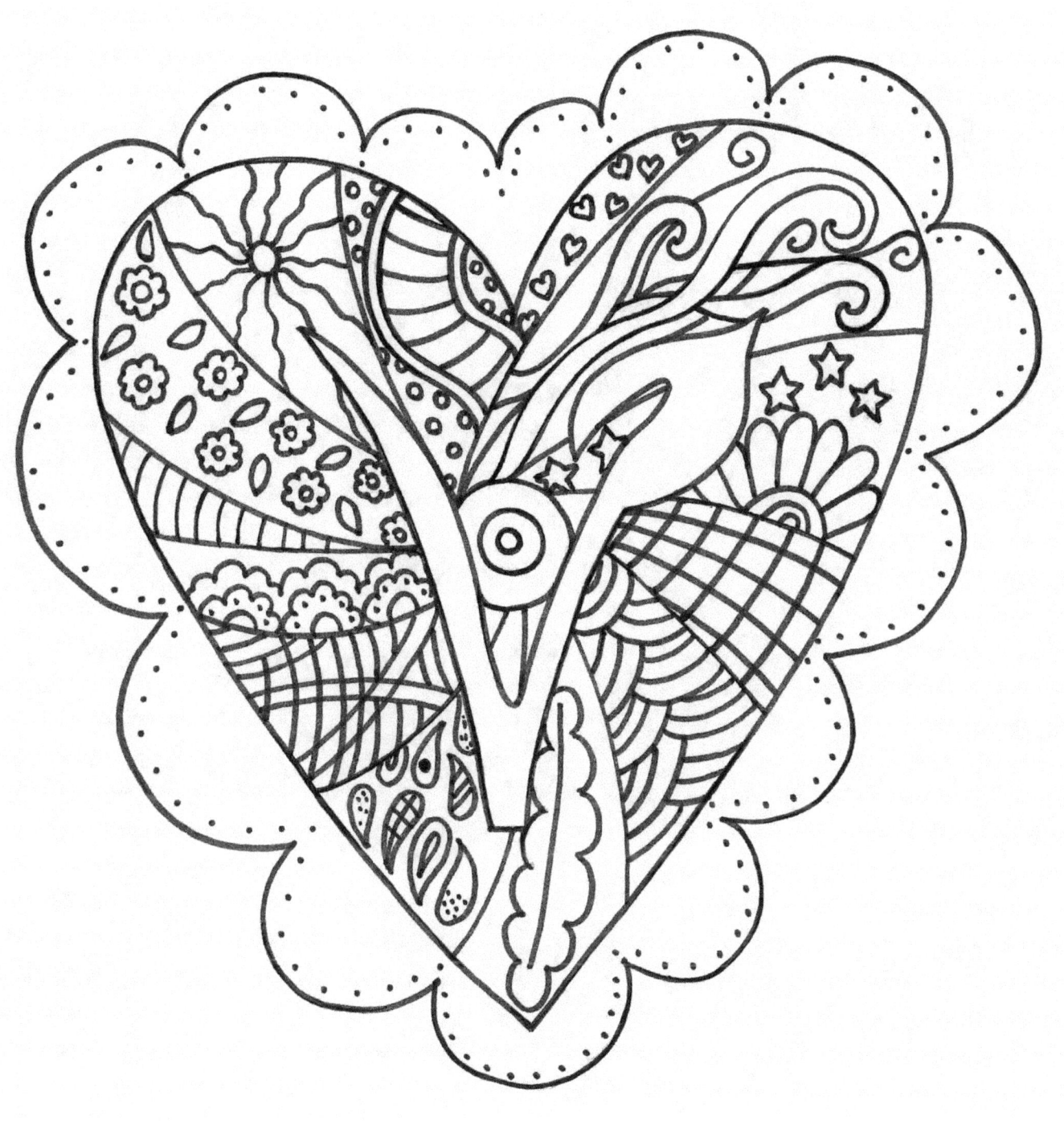

"After you have witnessed the reality, you can no longer look at a piece of steak, and simply think "yum"."

-Mango Wodzak-

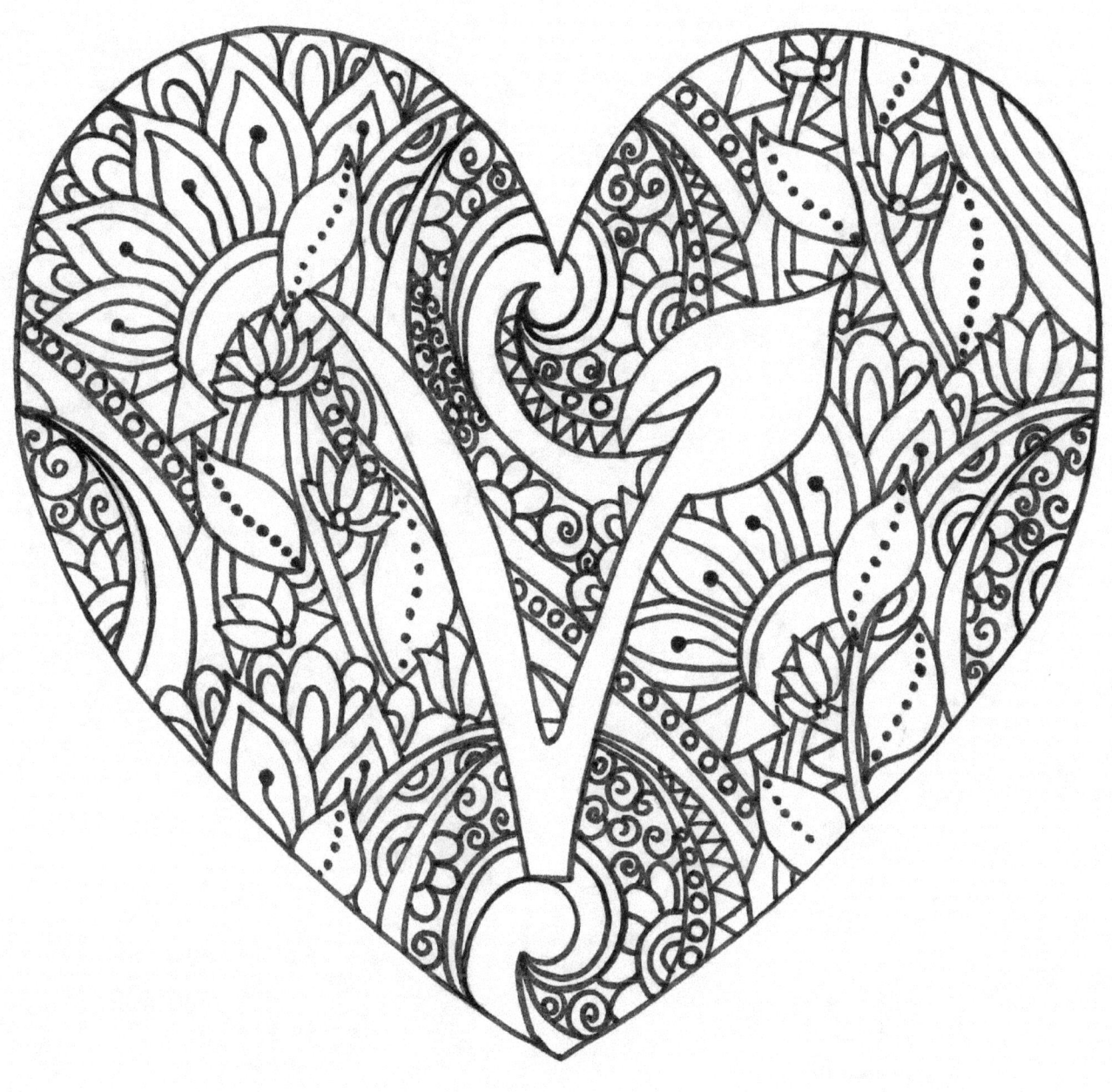

"The animals of the world exist for their own reason. They were not made for humans any more than black people were made for whites or women for men."

–Alice Walker–

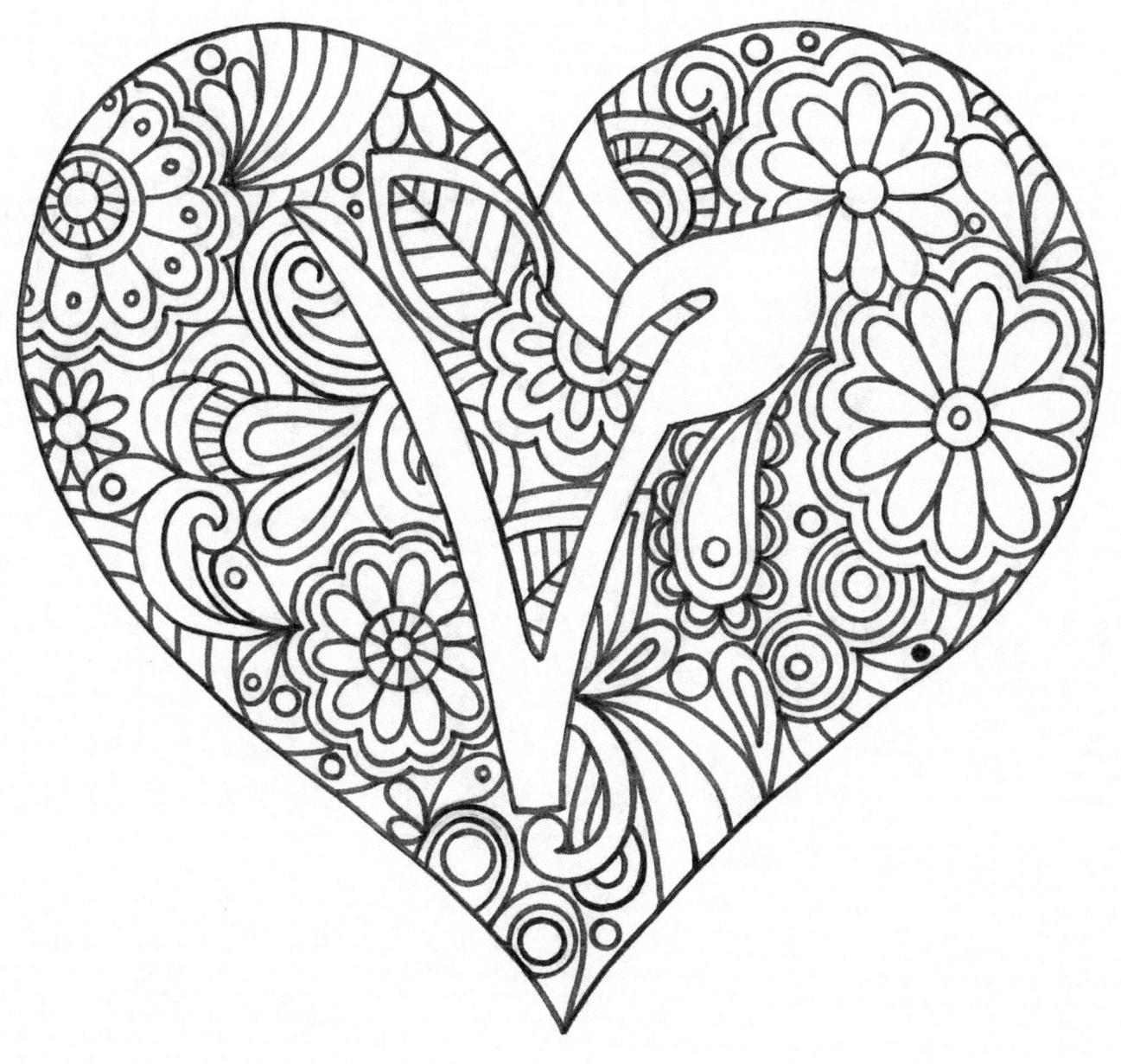

"Intelligence is the ability of a species to live in harmony
with its environment."
-Paul Watson-

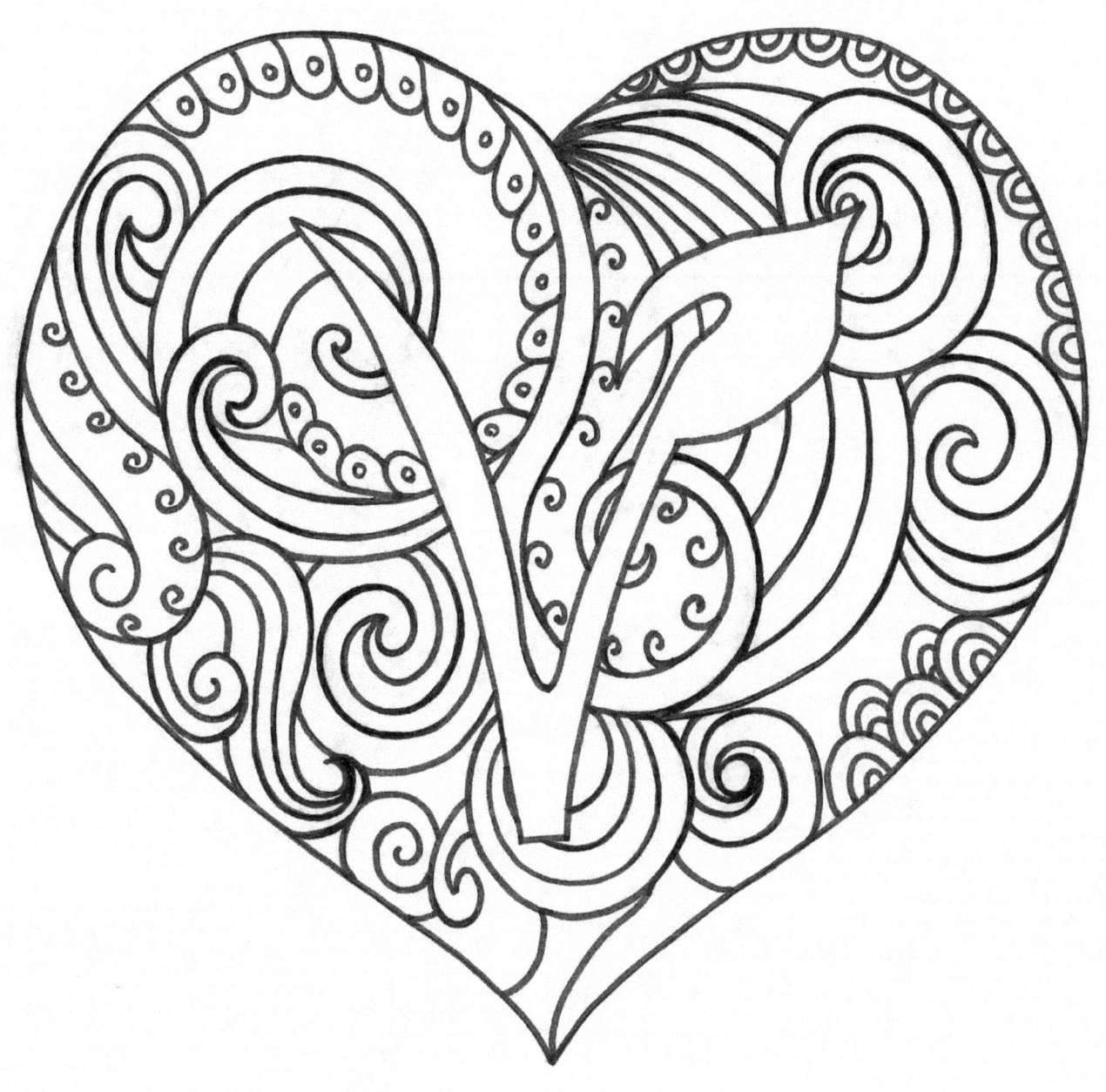

"I choose not to make a graveyard of my body for the rotting corpses of dead animals."

-George Bernard Shaw-

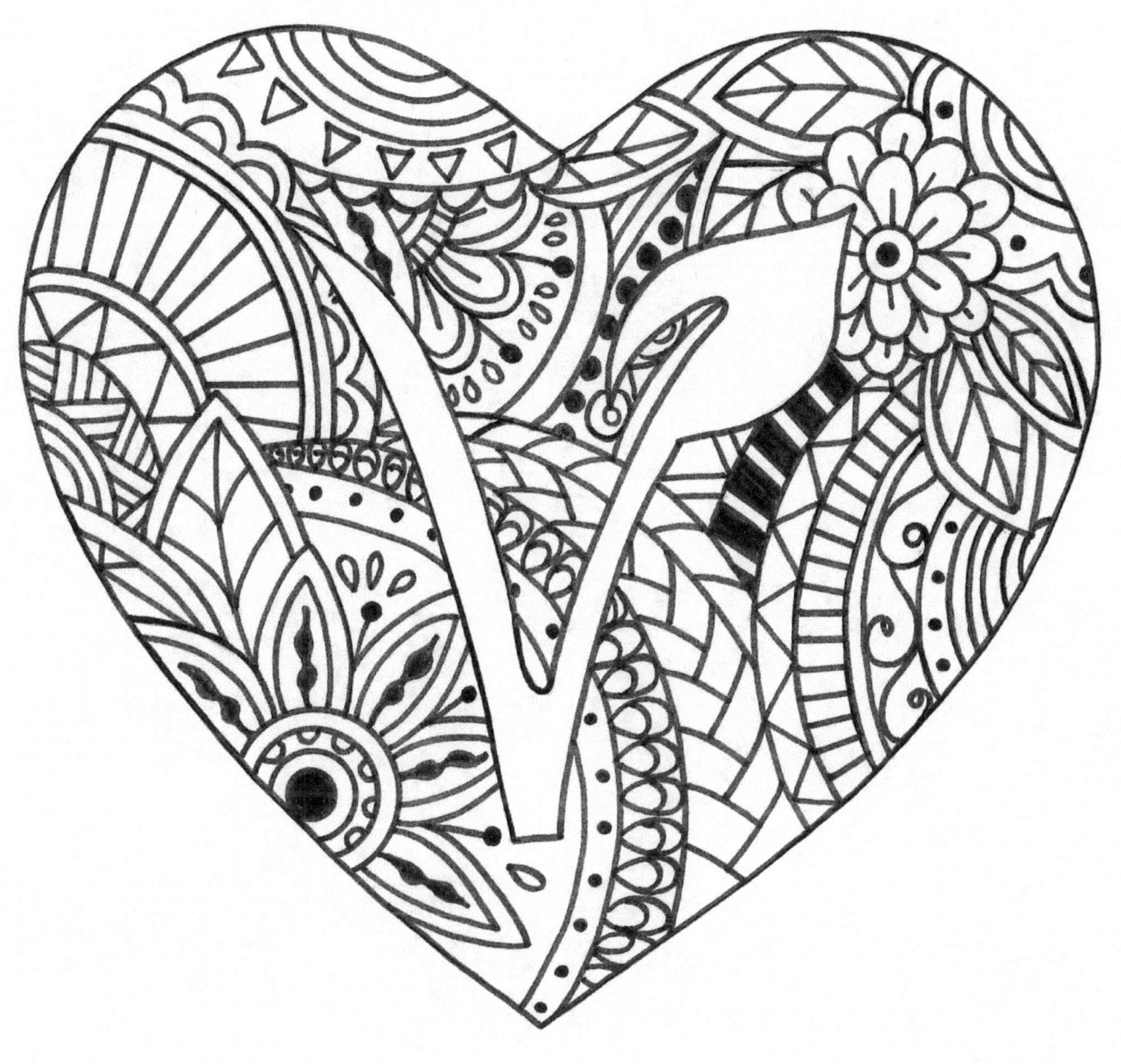

"All sentient beings should have at least one right –the

right not to be treated as property."

-Gary L. Francione-

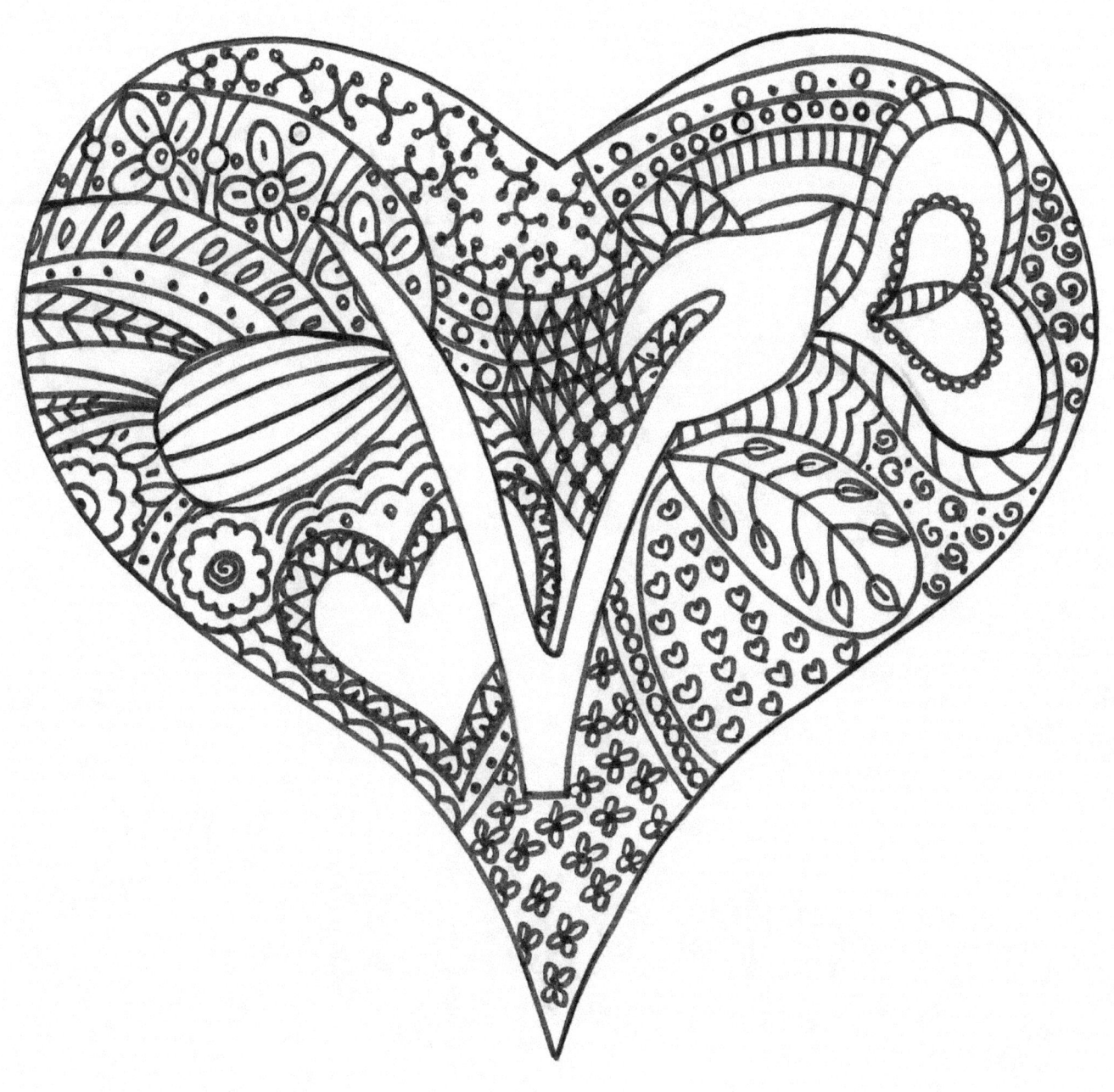

"There is something about veganism that is not easy, but the difficulty is not inherent in veganism, but in our culture." -Will Tuttle

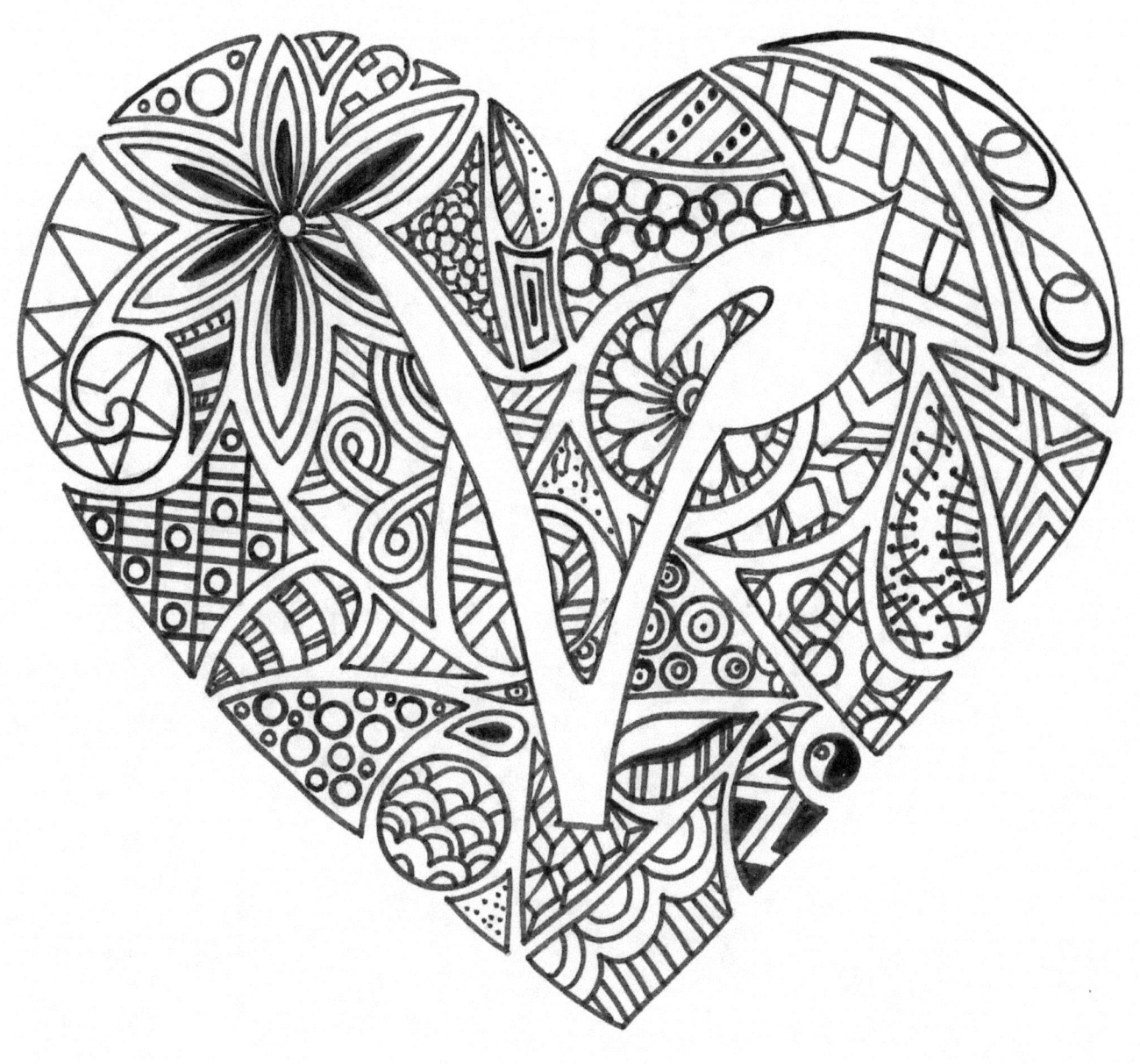

"What we must do is start viewing every cow, pig, chicken, monkey, rabbit, mouse, and pigeon as our family members."

-Gary Yourofsky-

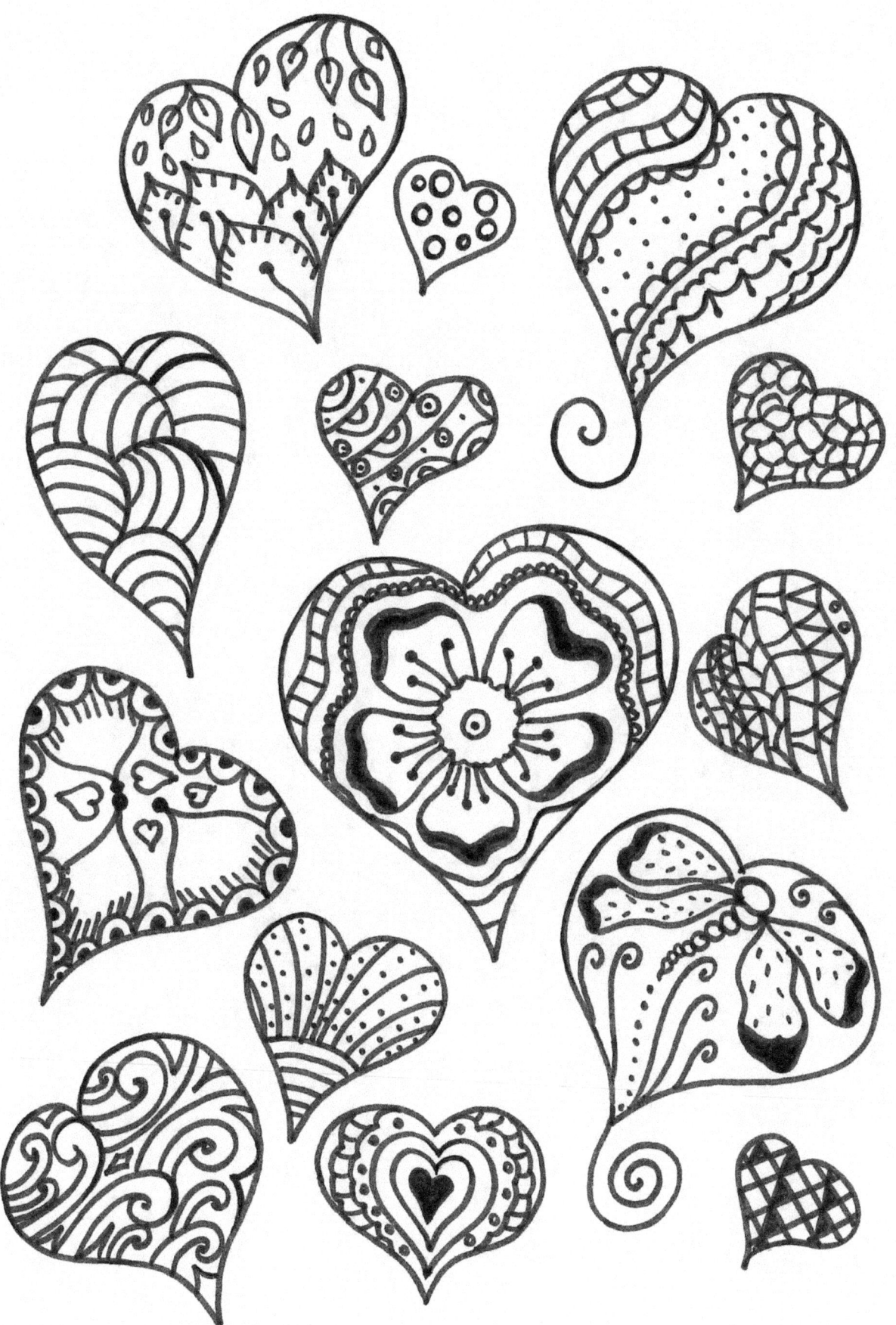

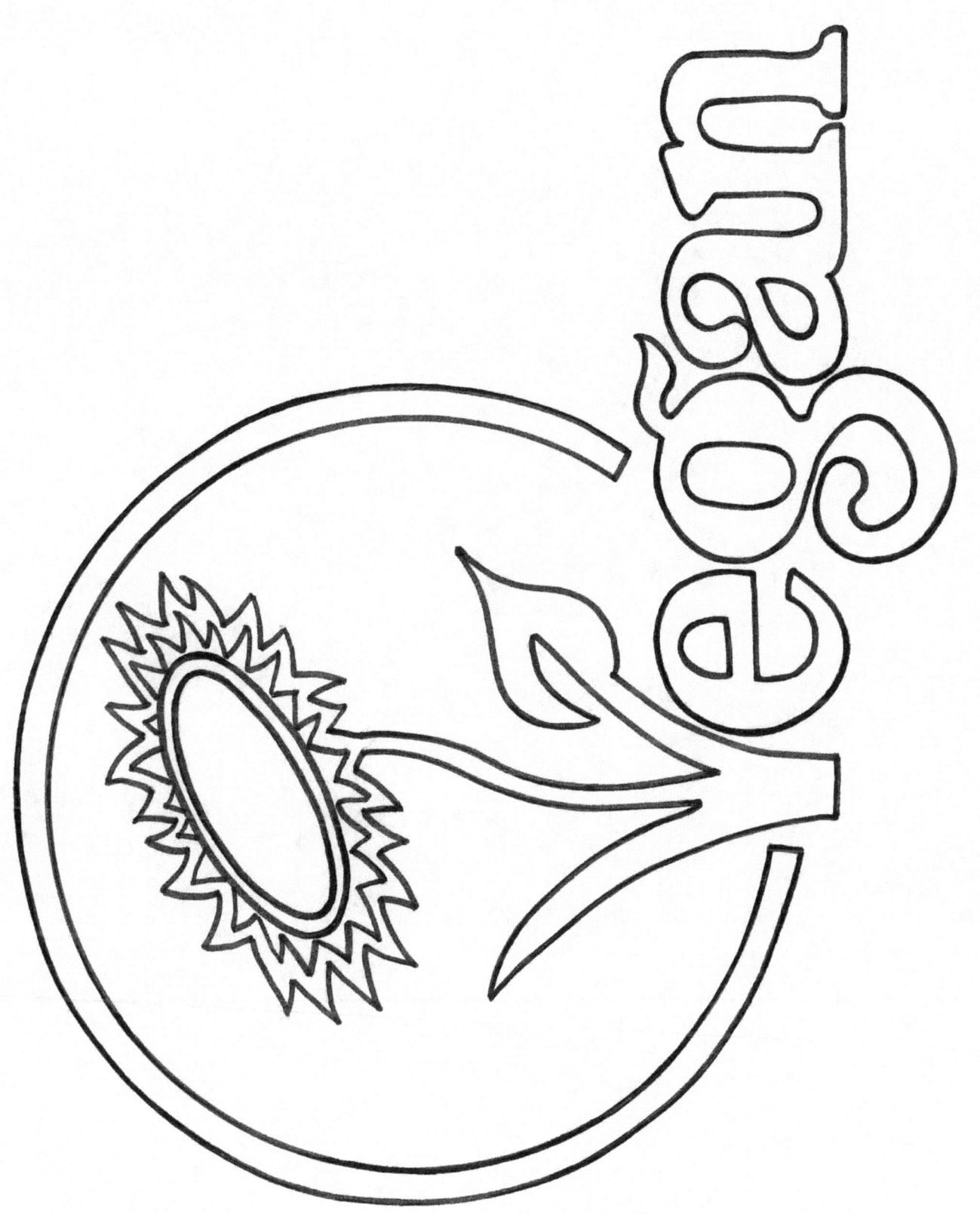

www.ingramcontent.com/pod-product-compliance
Lightning Source LLC
Chambersburg PA
CBHW081608200526
45169CB00021B/2727